ORANGE AND PURPLE = FedEx

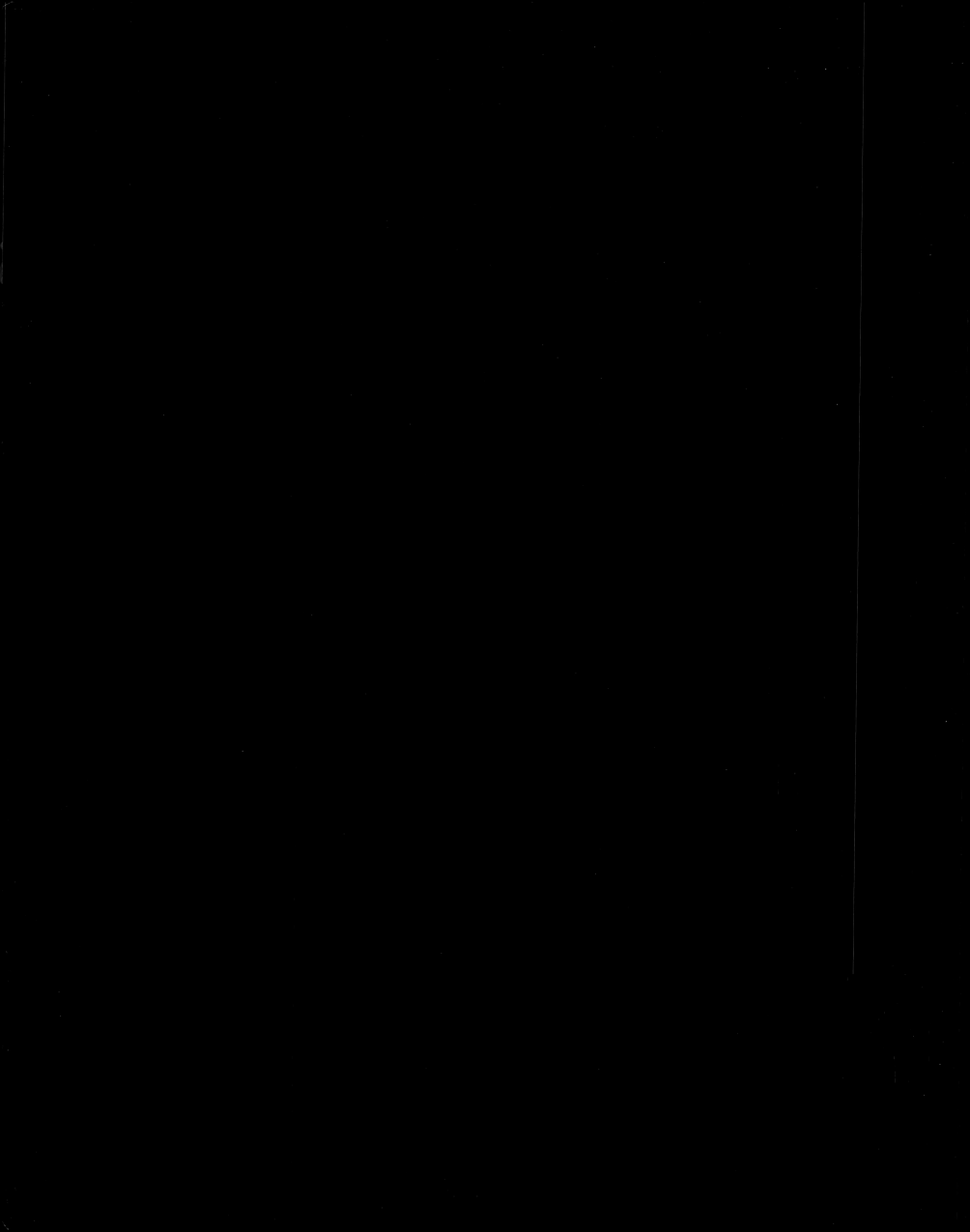

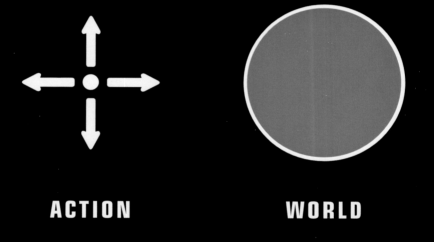

ACTION   WORLD   ACT

OBSTACL

FRIGH

THAT API

TAKE YO

YO

THOSE WHO CAN ACCEPT THE HARDSHIPS

WILL SAVOR THE TASTE OF VICTORY

THOSE WHO CAN ACCEPT THE HARDSHIPS

WILL SAVOR THE TASTE OF VICTORY

THOSE WHO CAN ACCEPT THE HARDSHIPS

WILL SAVOR THE TASTE OF VICTORY

THOSE WHO CAN ACCEPT THE HARDSHIPS

WILL SAVOR THE TASTE OF VICTORY

THOSE WHO CAN ACCEPT THE HARDSHIPS

WILL SAVOR THE TASTE OF VICTORY

THE PAST IS DEAD. FUTURE BELONGS THOSE WHO BELIEVE IN TRUTH OF THEIR IMAGINATION

YOU CAN'T TOUCH THE

AND STILL REMAIN AT

You will
the oth

If you never l

dreams are only dreams
until we awake

and make them come true

Keep things simple.

OBSTACLES ARE THOSE
FRIGHTFUL THINGS
THAT APPEAR WHEN YOU
TAKE YOUR MIND OFF
YOUR GOALS

1. Companies and brands have to show a commitment to the future, but in a relaxed and user friendly fashion.
2. At the same time, since people feel destabilized and need reassurance, companies and brands should promote their heritage.
3. If you use retro images, focus on the 50's, which resonate with every age group.

YOU CAN'T TOUCH THE STARS

AND STILL REMAIN AT HOME

Use numerals, not words.

THE PAST IS DEAD. THE
FUTURE BELONGS TO
THOSE

WHO BELIEVE IN THE
TRUTH OF THEIR OWN
IMAGINATION

You will never find the other ocean

you never leave the shore.

PRIDE IS KNOWING THAT TOO MUCH

IS NEVER ENOUGH

Keep things small.

4. Reward your customers with small self indulgences.
5. Use animals, pets and sports in your marketing communications.
6. Use lists, but keep the numbers small.
7. Avoid trite numbers like 5, 10 and 15. Instead, use prime numbers larger than five, which are "subliminally credible", such as 7, 11, 17 and 19.

THOSE WHO CAN ACCEPT THE HARDSHIPS

WILL SAVOR THE TASTE OF VICTORY

Guard against cynicism.

8. Eliminate suspense proactively; go beyond the guarantee. Tell people what to expect, then deliver on the expectations.
9. Be careful about teasing that involves uncertainty and suspense.
10. Don't make customers wait.
11. Always provide closure. Be careful about change, change creates stress.
12. Concentrate on customer service.

WINNERS ARE LOSERS

WITH A NEW ATTITUDE

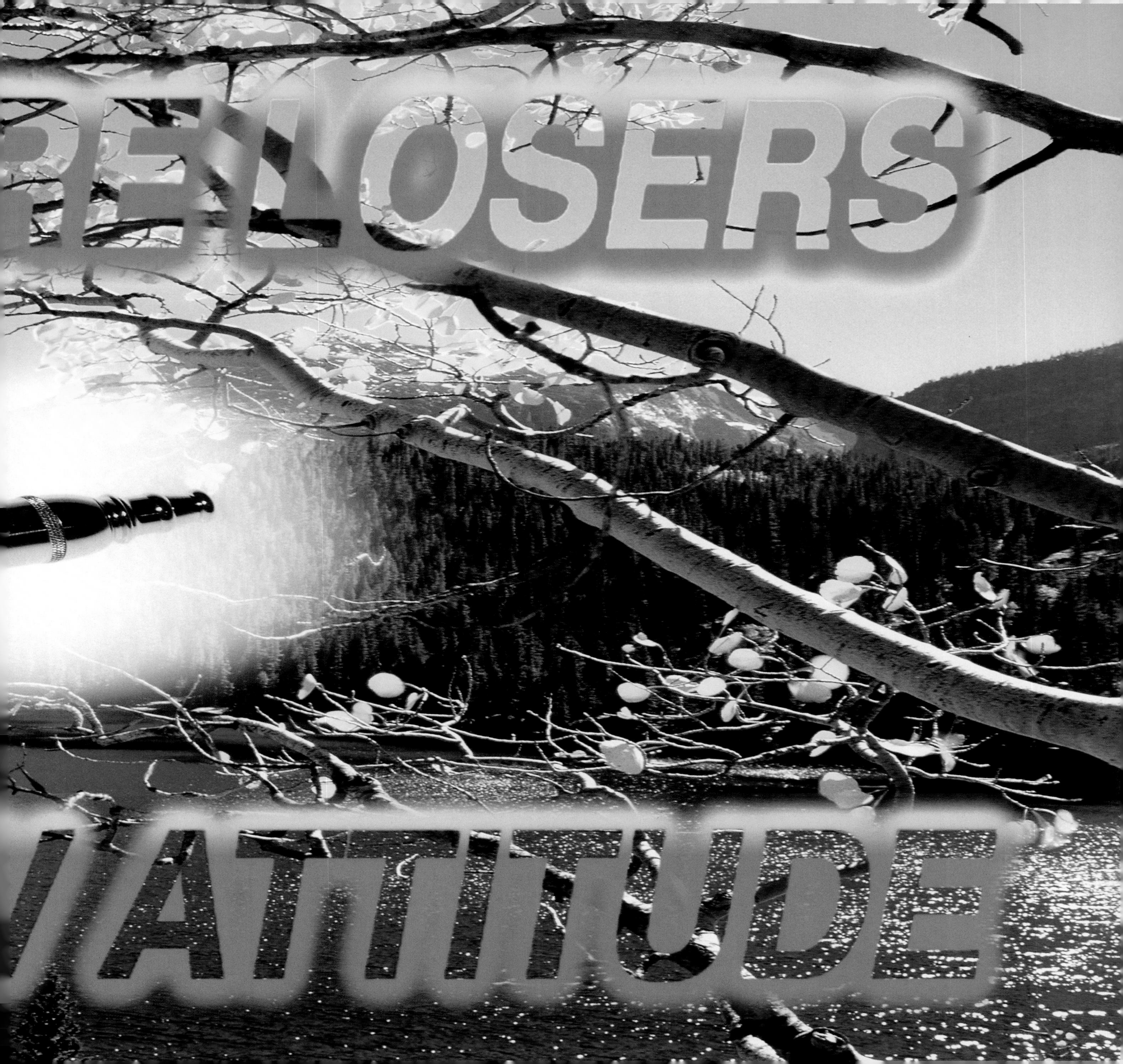
LOSERS
ATTITUDE

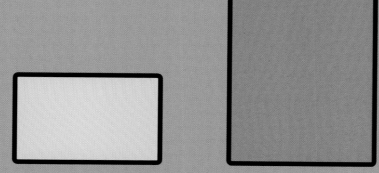

REGULAR
ACHIEVEMENT

MAXIMUM
ACHIEVEMENT

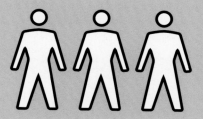

LOSERS

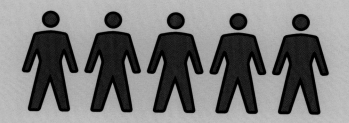

WINNERS

JUMP INTO YOURSELF!

CARING FOR OTHERS IS OUR JOB.
LOVING IT IS YOURS.

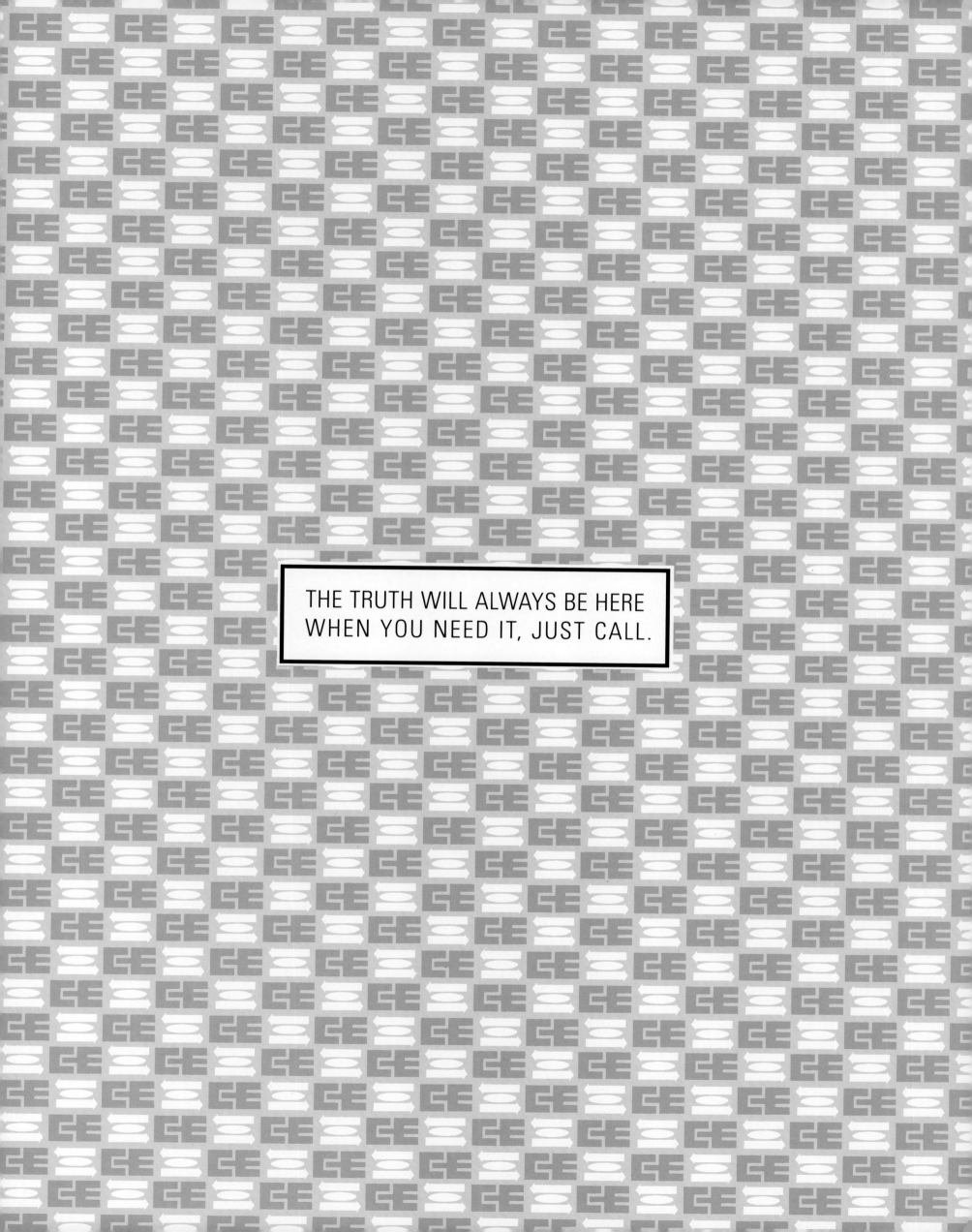

THE TRUTH WILL ALWAYS BE HERE
WHEN YOU NEED IT, JUST CALL.

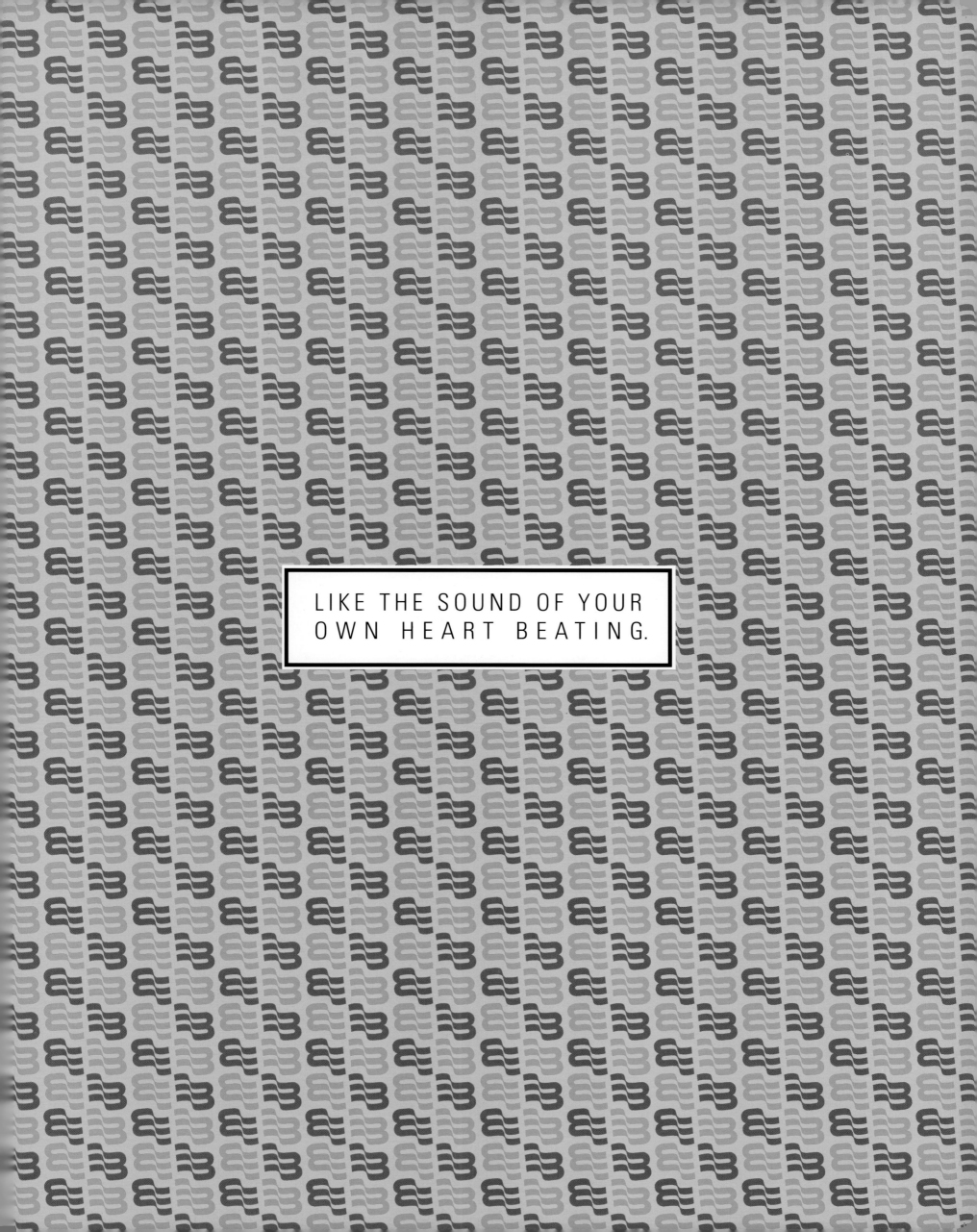

LIKE THE SOUND OF YOUR
OWN HEART BEATING.

WINNERS NEVER QUIT.
QUITTERS NEVER WIN.

START —

So let's get started . . .

Let me start with one **major warning.**

There is no need to put <u>any limitation on what is possible.</u>

Accumulate $50,000 in investments. Sleep soundly every night, argue with my spouse less than once per month.

But what if every area in your life from your career and finances to all your relationships and personal goals and accomplishments worked just the way you would design them if you were in complete and total control.

Develop your goals. Drop your expectations. Drop your expectations. Why are you always happy and excited, full of energy? Why don't you get angry or yell? How can you run a huge successful business conglomerate and yet find the time to spend 3 months every year traveling and exploring the world, never allowing anyone to call you about business?

Live your life around your dreams and you live life like the movie it was meant to be.

Know how you will look, how you will feel, what you will see and hear in your external world, after you have achieved your goals. Imagine that you can step out of your body. Imagine that your skin is like a dress or a jumpsuit and by simply un-zipping it you can free yourself. You step out unafraid. It is the new you. <u>The clean you.</u>

CONTINUE

There is no difference at all.

Become. Begin. Build. Invest. Create. Start. Complete. Work.

Know how you will look, how you will feel, what you will see and hear in your external world, after you have achieved your goals. Winning starts with beginning.

Know how you will look, how you will feel, what you will see and hear in your external world, after you have achieved your goals. Be in control.

Engage all your senses in describing the results you want. Where you is is where you is. The past is no longer real. Only the present moment is real. Your past is only a set of thoughts that could just as easily have come from a movie as from your own experiences.

What you need to do is dream.

Imagine setting out on a two week vacation with your car fully loaded but with no maps and no pre-determined destination. You'd be lost from the moment you left your driveway. No matter how fast you'd travel, you wouldn't be going anywhere.

Welcome to the exciting world of luxury rail service from the magnificent, historic Copper Canyon region of Mexico, populated by North America's most primitive native Indians, the Tarahumara.

Take an island. Surround it with the beach -- nearly 300 miles of it. Anchor it with a medieval fortress backed by a picturesque old town. Spread championship golf courses along dramatic coastlines. Lay mountains down the middle; top with lush rain forest. Lace with phosphorescent bays and mangrove forests.

People it all with U.S. citizens, proud of their home. Put it just a few hours' nonstop flight from most major U.S. cities. Picture Puerto Rico.

Your heart swells with anticipation. You have begun the 1996 Discovery of Golden Civilizations, a once-in-a-lifetime westward voyage to the distant lands of storybook legends, where new chapters are about to unfold.

The Northern Poetry of New England and Canada offers an abundance of rustic charm.

Your pulse slows. Your eyes open to morning glories.

Forget how old you are and remember how young you are.

Call your travel agent. Make yourself happy. Let yourself go.

Let me start with one major warning.

In truth, nothing is a big deal.

There is no need to put any limitation on what is possible.

TURN

There is, as you can see, no such thing as trying. Trying, therefore, is lying.

CONTINUE →

You hear your childhood friends playing games you used to play. They're transparent now and all are free from the constraints and bondage of their skins. Everyone gazes at the waterfalls and patterns of the ripples like the flicking of a fire. All are mesmerized by their own beauty. The sound of a distant tree. A telephone rings but no one answers for the answers are all now clear as day, a bright shiny day that could be anywhere -- in your apartment or in a distant mountain valley. There is no difference at all.

Put the blunt down just for a second. Don't get me wrong. It's not a new method. Inhale, exhale, just got an ounce in the mail. I like the blunt but my double barrel bong is getting me stoned. There's water inside, don't spill it, smells like shit on the carpet.
Goes down smooth when I get a hit of the funky smelly green shit. I sing my song all night long as I take hits from the bong.

As I sit back and look where I used to be a crook, doing whatever it took, from snatching chains to pocket books, a big bad mutherfucker on the wrong road. I got some drugs, tried to get the avenue sold. I want it all, from the Rolexes to the Lexus. Getting paid is all I expected. Mother didn't get me what I want. What the fuck. Now I got a glock making mutherfuckers duck. Shit is real and hungry's how I feel. I rob and steal because the money's got that whip appeal.

Kickin' niggas down the step just for wreck. Any repercussion leads to niggas gettin' wet. The infrared's at your head. Real steady. Better get your guns 'cause I'm ready.

Try to fight the system.

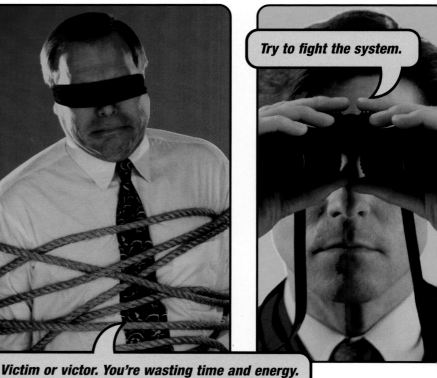

Victim or victor. You're wasting time and energy.

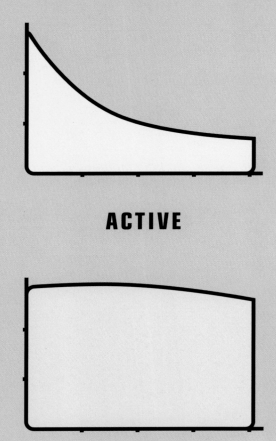

ACTIVE

PROACTIVE

COWARD 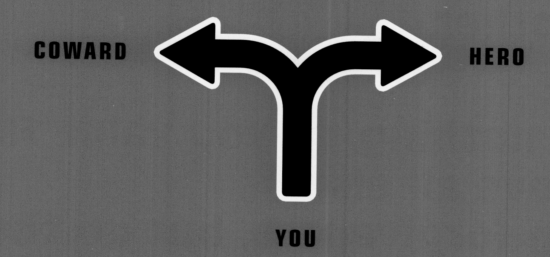 HERO

YOU

You can save the lives of hundreds of people, but you must kill your own mother.

Do you:
A. ☐ Do nothing, as you value family above all else.
B. ☐ Beg forgiveness, but do the deed.

You discover a way of streamlining the business and of making everything run more cheaply and efficiently, but everyone else is very happy with things as they are.

Do you:
A. ☐ Ignore their feelings and do what is best for the company
B. ☐ Go along with the consensus of the group.
C. ☐ Enlist the help of an unbiased third party.

You stumble upon evidence that your boyfriend or girlfriend is cheating on you, but he or she is just about to take you on a trip that you've been waiting for your whole life.

Do you:
A. ☐ Wait and confront them during the trip.
B. ☐ Confront them now and risk the trip.
C. ☐ Enjoy the trip and hope that it was just a temporary thing.

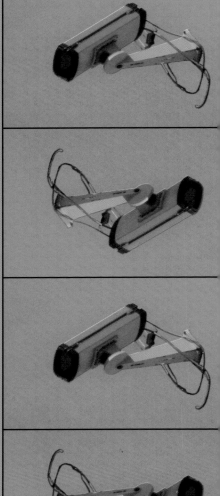

You're in line at the train station when a little man, feigning innocence, cuts in line in front of you.

Do you:
A. ☐ Ignore him, as it's not really worth making a scene.
B. ☐ Shout out "Hey Buddy, the end of the line is back there".
C. ☐ Reciprocate – and cut in front him.

You can see into the future, and you have the opportunity to tell your best friends what will happen to them and when.

Do you:
A. ☐ Lie to them, and tell them only the good news.
B. ☐ Keep it to yourself.
C. ☐ Let them have an honest opportunity to deal with the truth, however unpleasant.

You've put years of work into a project, and your best friend steals your idea.

Do you:
A. ☐ Sue them, as they obviously can't be a real friend.
B. ☐ Offer to become partners.
C. ☐ Do nothing, as your friendship will outlast this.

You're on an airplane - the beautiful woman or man seated next to you falls asleep and starts to lean on you.

Do you:
A. ☐ Smoothly put your arm around him or her.
B. ☐ Wedge a pillow in between the two of you as a divider.
C. ☐ Wake the person up and then return to your reading.

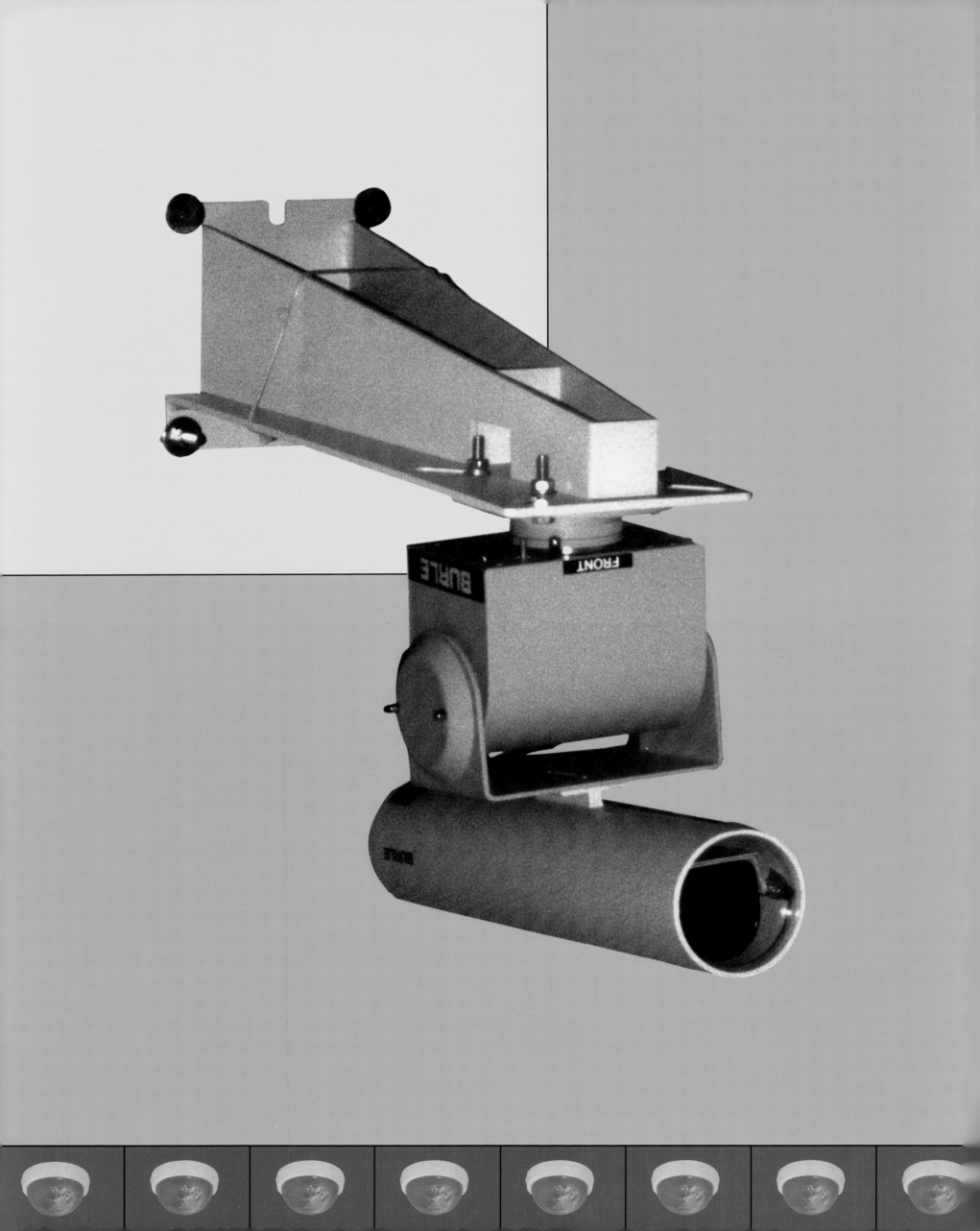

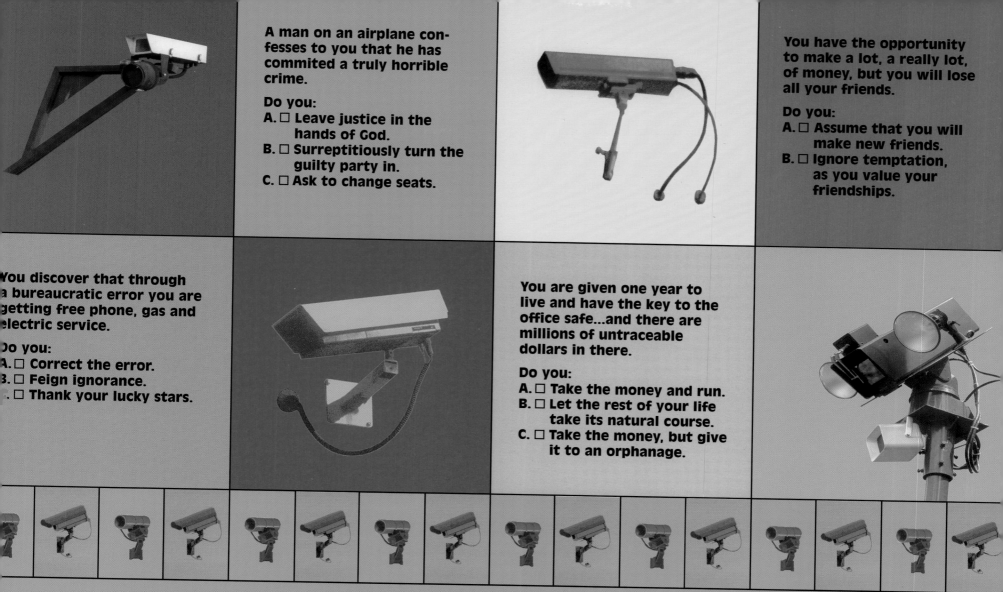

A man on an airplane confesses to you that he has commited a truly horrible crime.

Do you:
A. ☐ Leave justice in the hands of God.
B. ☐ Surreptitiously turn the guilty party in.
C. ☐ Ask to change seats.

You have the opportunity to make a lot, a really lot, of money, but you will lose all your friends.

Do you:
A. ☐ Assume that you will make new friends.
B. ☐ Ignore temptation, as you value your friendships.

You discover that through a bureaucratic error you are getting free phone, gas and electric service.

Do you:
A. ☐ Correct the error.
B. ☐ Feign ignorance.
C. ☐ Thank your lucky stars.

You are given one year to live and have the key to the office safe...and there are millions of untraceable dollars in there.

Do you:
A. ☐ Take the money and run.
B. ☐ Let the rest of your life take its natural course.
C. ☐ Take the money, but give it to an orphanage.

You are accosted in a dark alley by 3 armed youths who demand your wallet, but you are, unbeknown to them, carrying a powerful semi-automatic weapon.

Do you:
A. ☐ Administer justice. Shoot first and ask questions later, it's self defense.
B. ☐ Pull your weapon but leave the scene peacefully.
C. ☐ Give up your wallet and avoid the risk of violent confrontation.

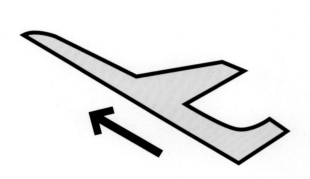

HOPE   **DESPAIR**

L

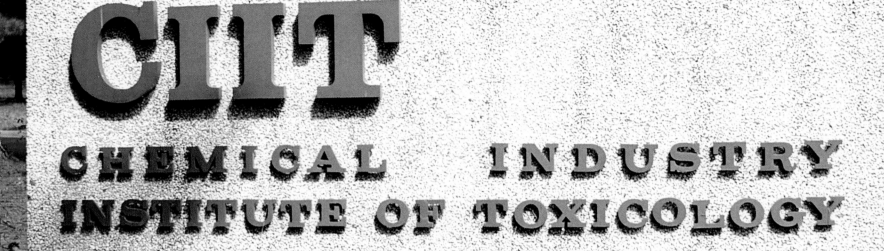

CIIT
CHEMICAL INDUSTRY
INSTITUTE OF TOXICOLOGY

AMERICAN ASSOCIATION OF
TEXTILE CHEMISTS AND COLORISTS
TECHNICAL CENTER

The University of North Carolina Center for Public Television

- North Carolina State Education Assistance Authority
- International Visitors Council

CIBA–GEIGY

Biotechnology Facility

IBM

↑
Main Site
→
B/632 Education Ctr

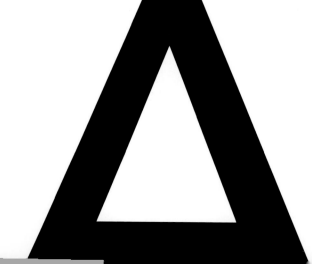

BEFORE   **AFTER**

Apply C   Only To
Affected A   Area. May
Be Too Int   tense For
Some Vie   ewers. Do
Not Sta   mp. For
Recreatio   onal Use
Only. If C   Condition
Persists,   Consult
Your Phys   sician. No
User-Ser   rviceable
Parts   Inside.
Freshest   If Eaten
Before D   Date On
Carton. S   ubject To
Change   Without
Notice. S   Simulated
Pictur   e. Any
Resemblan   ce To Real
Persons   Living Or
Dead Is   s Purely
Coincid   dental.
Contents M   May Settle
During S   hipment.

All Models Over 18
Years Of Age. This
Product Is Meant For
Educational Purposes
Only. Void Where
Prohibited. Some
Assembly Required.
List Each Check
Separately By Bank
Number. Batteries
Not Included. Use
Only As Directed. No
Other Warranty
Expressed Or Implied.
Do Not Use While
Operating A Motor
Vehicle Or Heavy
Equipment. Times
Approximate. Postage
Will Be Paid By
Addressee. This Is
Not An Offer To Sell
Securities.

Your Canceled Check Is Your Receipt. No Purchase Necessary. Employees And Their Families Are Not Eligible. Sanitized For Your Protection. Beware Of Dog. Contestants Have Been Briefed On Some Questions Before The Show. Limited Time Offer, Call Now To Ensure Prompt Delivery. You Must Be Present To Win. Slightly Higher West Of The Mississippi. Avoid Contact With Skin. Shading Within A Garment May Occur. Keep Away From Fire Or Flames. Replace With Same Type. Approved For Veterans. Price Does Not Include Taxes. No Solicitors. No Alcohol, Dogs Or Horses. Some Equipment Shown Is Optional. Reproduction Strictly Prohibited. Driver Does Not Carry Cash.

No Postage Necessary If Mailed In The United States. Please Remain Seated Until The Ride Has Come To A Complete Stop. Breaking Seal Constitutes Acceptance Of Agreement. For Off-Road Use Only. As Seen On TV. One Size Fits All. Many Suitcases Look Alike. Colors May Fade. Slippery When Wet. For Office Use Only. Drop In Any Mailbox. Edited For Television. Post Office Will Not Deliver Without Postage. List Was Current At Time Of Printing. Return To Sender, No Forwarding Order On File, Unable To Forward. Not Responsible For Direct, Indirect, Incidental Or Consequential Damages Resulting From Any Defect, Error Or Failure To Perform. At Participating Locations/Stores Only. Penalty For Private Use. Lost Ticket Pays Maximum Rate. Substantial Penalty For Early Withdrawal. Falling Rock. Restaurant Package, Not For Resale.

Do Not Write Below This Line

Do Not Write Below This Line.

Use Only In A Well-Ventilated Area. Do Not
Fold, Spindle Or Mutilate. Objects In Mirror
May Be Closer Than They Appear.
This Supersedes All Previous Notices.

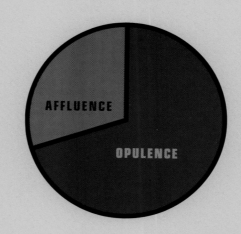

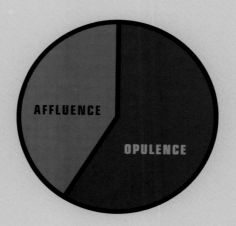

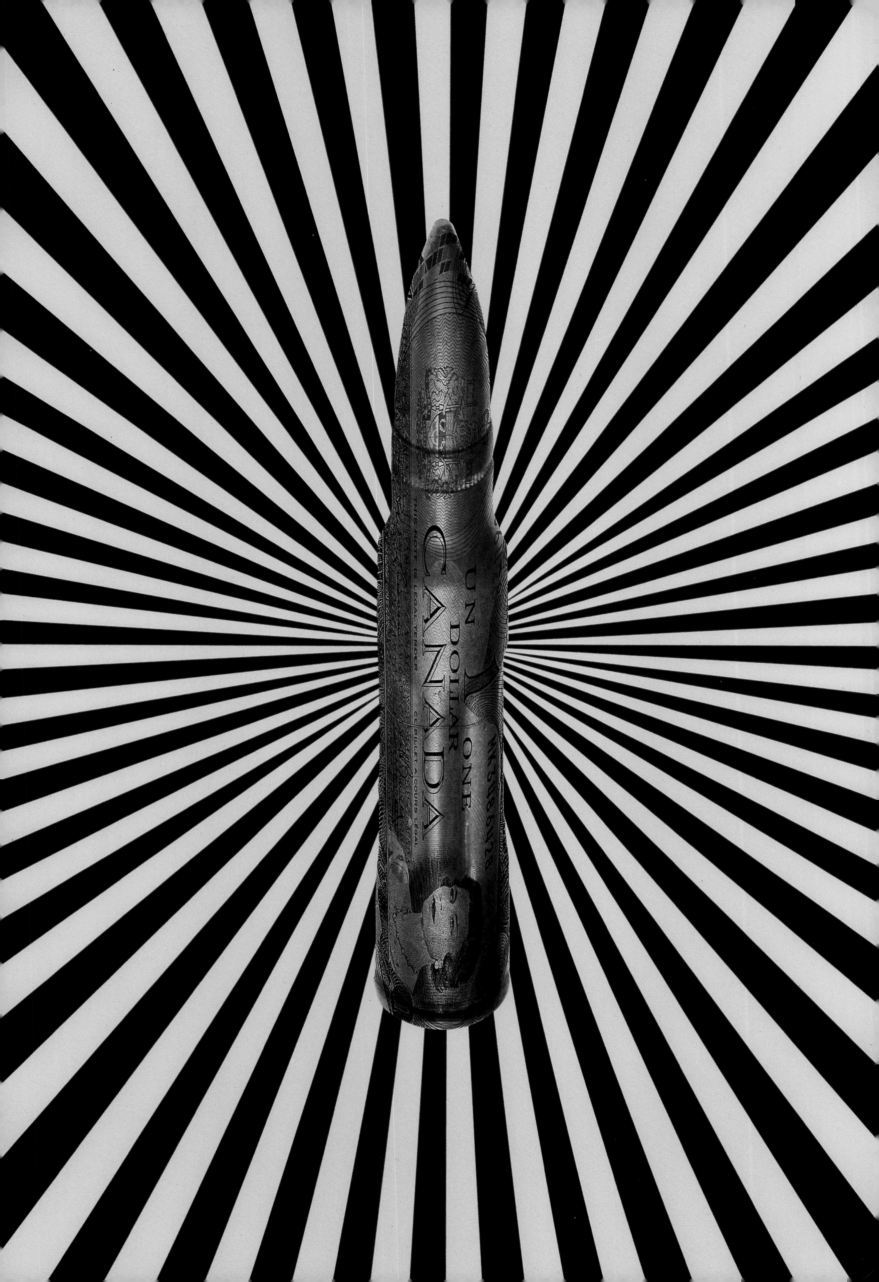

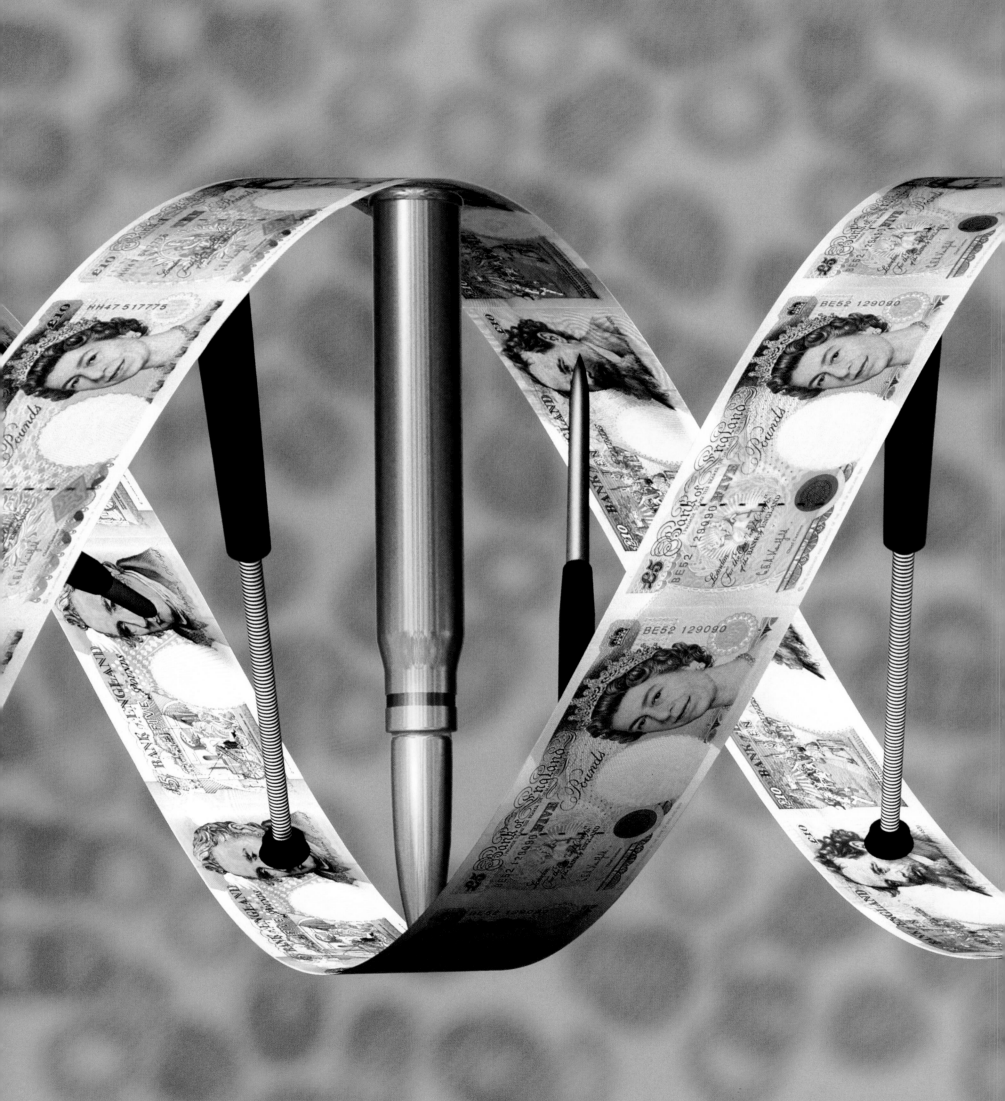

SERIAL NO.
606590

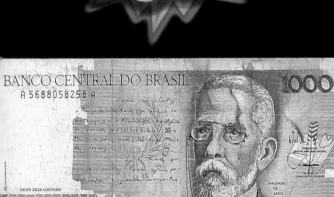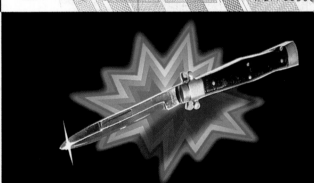

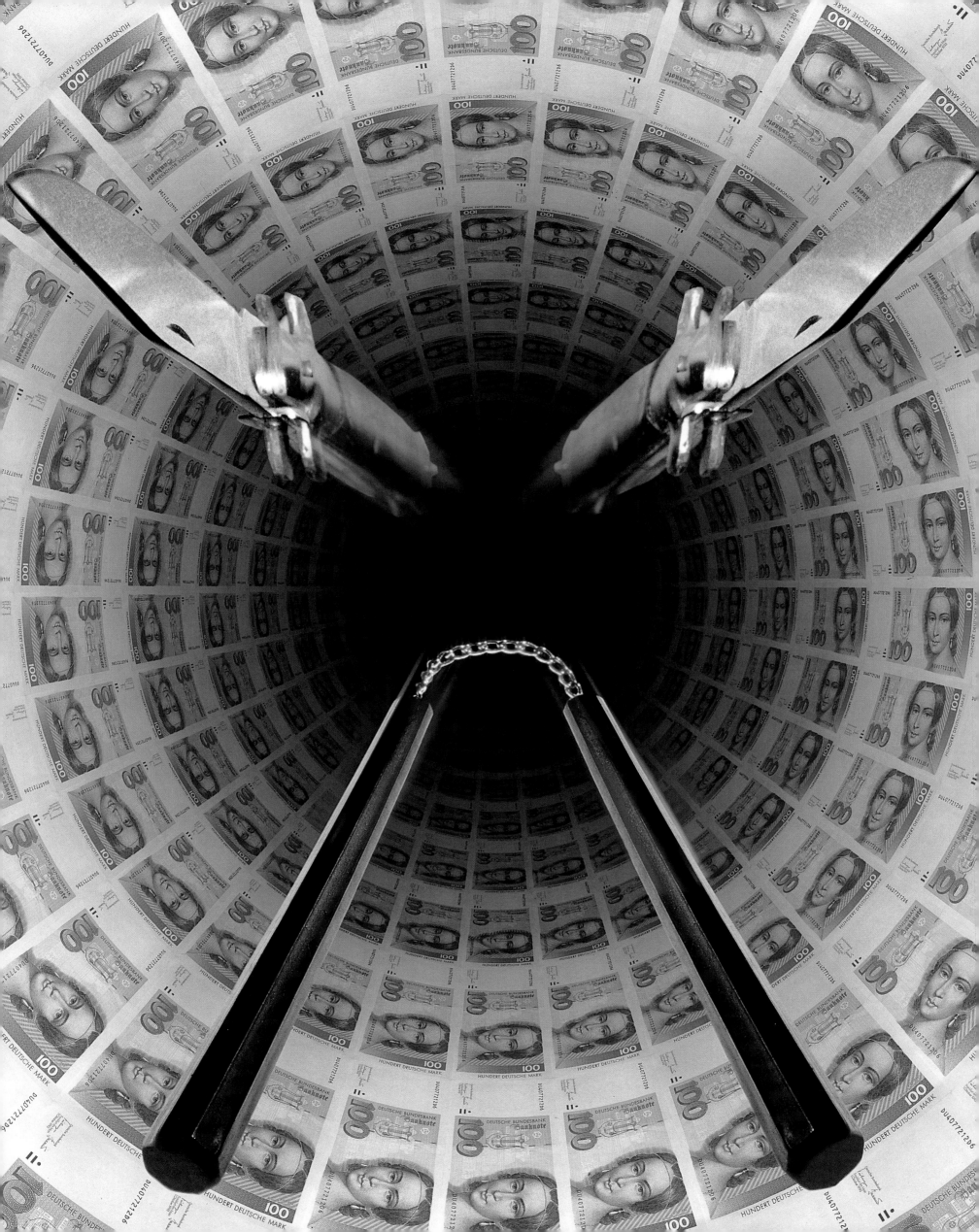

ACTION + WORLD = ACTION WORLD / BETTER LIVING THROUGH CHEMISTRY

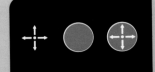

Red Barn / Hemostat Clip, 1995

Palm Tree / $100 Bill, 1995

Vertical strip —
Hong Kong / Death Bong, 1995
Grid clockwise from top left:
Monument Valley / Syringe, 1995
Liberty / Bat Roach Clip, 1995
Big Ben / Coke Snorter, 1995
Acid Trip, 1995

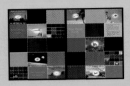

Text found on Internet

Lake & Leaves / Metal Pipe, 1995

REGULAR ACHIEVEMENT / MAXIMUM ACHIEVEMENT

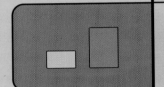

Blockade, Jacksonville, FLA, 1997

Swingers, 1978

3 Options, Jacksonville, FLA, 1997
On the Beach, Jacksonville, FLA, 1997

Squeeze Play, Jacksonville, FLA,
1997

Cafeteria, Montserrat Monestary,
Spain, 1996

WINNERS / LOSERS - SUPEREGO: YOU ARE A COMPANY AND ITS PRODUCT

Sleep, 1997

Pride, 1997

Ecstasy, 1997

Love, 1997

WINNERS NEVER QUIT / QUITTERS NEVER WIN

"Your Action World" text compiled
and written by David Byrne

WINNERS NEVER QUIT.
QUITTERS NEVER WIN.

ACTIVE / PROACTIVE

Bellybutton Camouflage, Burma, 1995

Protection, Mexico, 1997

Fade Out, Salamanca, Spain, 1998

Blocked, Las Vegas, 1997

Hallway, Vatican City, 1997
In Your Corner, 1994

Underground Storage, Nevada, 1997
Abstract Art, Santa Monica, 1997

Pastoral Landscape, Heathrow
Lounge, 1997
Available, Valencia, Spain, 1998

Road Map, 1995
The Future, California, 1996

Pilgrimage, Las Vegas, 1997

YOU - COWARD - HERO

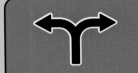

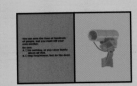

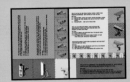

Surveillance Camera photos by David Byrne, 1994-98
12 Moral Questions text by David Byrne

HOPE / DESPAIR

Gardens of Stone, Research Triangle, North Carolina, 1992

BEFORE / AFTER

U.S. Freeway Overpasses, 1979
Text found on Internet

AFFLUENCE / OPULENCE - STAIRWAY TO HEAVEN

 Ce Bullet a Cours Légal, 1996

 Textura Nova, 1996
Achievement!, 1996

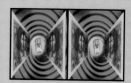 2 Yuan & A Boxcutter, 1996

 Installation, Public Toilet, Tenderloin District, San Francisco, 1997
Zabesto!, 1996

 Blue Blood, 1996

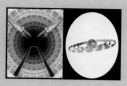 Deutsche Traum, 1996
Homemade Personal Weapon, 1996

 National Security, 1996

 Installation, Public Toilet, Tenderloin District, San Francisco, 1997
Democracy, 1996

DESIGN: SAGMEISTER INC., NEW YORK

Project Coordinator: Sarah Caplan
Executive Producer: Marco Puntin
Produced by Lipanje Puntin, Trieste, Italy

with the contribution of illy

LIPANJEPUNTIN
ARTECONTEMPORANEA
Via Diaz, 4 34121 Trieste Italy Tel.+39.040308099 Fax+39.040308287
Http://www.copeco.it/lipuarte · Email: lipuarte@tin.it

Thanks to Bob Bowen Studios, Geraldine Lucid (digital assistance), Esteban Mauchi, Tony Triano (prints), Laumont Labs, Yuji Yoshimoto (doll fabrication), Adelle Lutz, Nicholas Carter,

Elisabetta d'Erme, Franco Di Lauro, Bridget Shields, John Thomas, Andrea Fonzar, Cristina Lipanje, Paola Magni, Ariella Risch, Amanda Vertovese, Carlo Bach, Michele Concina

Chronicle Books
85 Second Street
San Francisco, CA 94105

www.chroniclebooks.com

CHRONICLE BOOKS
SAN FRANCISCO

Distributed in Canada by
Raincoast Books
8680 Cambie Street
Vancouver, BC V6P 6M9